MAPS & MAZES

a first guide to mapmaking

Gillian Chapman & Pam Robson

THE MILLBROOK PRESS

To Daphne Butler, our Editor

Visualization and map design: Gillian Chapman
Photography: Rupert Horrox

First published in Great Britain in 1993
by Simon & Schuster Young Books

Published in the United States by
The Millbrook Press
2 Old New Milford Rd.
Brookfield, CT 06804

Printed in Hong Kong

Library of Congress Cataloging-in-Publication
   Data
Chapman, Gillian.
   Maps & Mazes/Gillian Chapman & Pam
   Robson.
      p.   cm.
   Provides a visual introduction to the
principles of maps and mazes, with projects
children can create on their own.
   ISBN 1–56294–405–3 (lib. ed.)
   ISBN 1–56294–715–X (tr. ed.)
   1. Map drawing–Juvenile literature.
I. Robson, Pam, II. Title. III. Title: Maps and
mazes.
GA130.C46   1993   93–1234
526–dc20   CIP
                                                              AC

C o n t e n t s

Maps Have Meaning	4 - 5
Simple Plans	6 - 7
3D to 2D	8 - 9
Fixing Position	10 - 11
Mazes	12 - 13
Direction	14 - 15
Scale	16 - 17
Simple Mapmaking	18 - 19
Using a Grid	20 - 21
Contours & Coasts	22 - 23
Latitude & Longitude	24 - 25
Reading Signs	26 - 27
Shape & Size	28 - 29
Information Maps	30 - 31
Word List	32

The First Maps

When the first maps were made, finding your way—however short the journey—was a hazardous adventure. Most people did not know what lay just over the horizon. And early maps were not very accurate.

Jerusalem

Maps show the ideas of those who draw them. Maps drawn in the Middle Ages show the Earth as a flat disk with Jerusalem at the center.

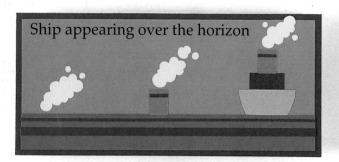

Ship appearing over the horizon

People believed for a long time that the Earth was flat. They gradually realized that it was round, by watching ships appear and disappear over the horizon. They understood that this could only happen if the Earth's surface was curved.

Five hundred years ago European adventurers sailed westward across

▲ Some of the earliest maps were plans like this view of a garden, painted on the wall of an ancient Egyptian tomb.
Reproduced by courtesy of the Trustees of the British Museum.

the Atlantic Ocean and reached America. The journey took months. Today supersonic aircraft can reach London from New York in less than four hours. And we know much more about the Earth and its features than people did hundreds of years ago.

The Earth

Only photographs taken from satellites show the true shape of the Earth. The Earth is a **sphere** spinning around on its own **axis**. This is why we have day and night. The axis is tilted, and the Earth travels around the sun in an **elliptical orbit**.

The Earth as a Globe

A globe is the same shape as the Earth but scaled down in size. Because a globe is a ball, it gives a good picture of the shape and position of land masses and oceans.

A globe has a network of lines printed on it. These are called lines of **latitude** and **longitude**. Using this network, every place on Earth can be given a fixed position.

The Earth as a Map

Copying a spherical globe with its lines of latitude and longitude onto a flat sheet of paper has always been a problem for mapmakers. In whatever way it is done, the shape and position of the land masses become distorted.

Using Maps

People use maps because they are very easy to carry around and can show the whole world or only a very small portion of it. A book containing maps of all the countries of the world is called an **atlas**.

People need different maps for different purposes. A traveler in a car needs a road map, a sailor needs a **chart**, and someone who is planning a walk in the mountains needs a very detailed map of the area.

Bird's-Eye View

When you look at things around you, you are seeing them from your own viewpoint. Someone taller or smaller than you will see the same things from a different viewpoint. A worm popping out of the ground looks up, and views objects from below. A bird flying high in the sky looks down, and views objects from above.

Imagine yourself as a bird sitting at the top of a high tree. You have a bird's-eye view of the world below. In the story opposite a bird is watching a cat from the top of a tree. The bird has a bird's-eye view of everything in the garden. The cat prowling around the garden cannot see the bird—it has a different viewpoint.

Viewed from above, everything in the garden looks quite different. The bird sees a plan of each object. It is unable to see how high each object is. The cat sees everything from below. It can see how tall everything is.

Plans and Pictures

The objects in the pictures below are all in the plan on the opposite page. In the top row you can see them as plans, just as the bird sees them. The bottom row shows how the cat sees them. Can you match each object with its plan?

On the facing page is the story about a cat and a bird. Read the story and follow the cat's paw marks on the plan.

"Where's That Cat?"

Out came the hungry cat . . . through the cat flap. It passed the trash can . . . crossed the lawn . . . and went around the tree. Over the wall . . . and back under the hedge . . . toward the bird feeder, next to the pond . . . Splash! In went the wet cat, through the cat flap. . . . And down flew the bird, laughing.

From the top of the tree the bird follows the cat's movements by observing the **landmarks** that the cat passes close to. The landmarks are the noticeable objects like the bird feeder and the trash can. By pinpointing a landmark and describing where a person or object is in relation to it—above, below, beside, and so on—you can explain to someone else exactly where that person or object is.

Make a Story Plan

Write a story about a short journey. You could retell a story from a book you have read recently. Then make a simple plan showing the journey taken in the story, sketching in the route and any landmarks passed along the way.

Where's That Cat?
Out came the hungry cat....
through the cat flap.
It passed the trash can....
crossed the lawn....and
went around the tree.
Over the wall... and
under the

rockery

house

pond

wall

tree

hedge

Looking at 2-D Pictures

You have already discovered that a bird's-eye view is a plan of an object. The bird at the top of the tree sees a flat shape when it looks down on the top of the bird feeder. It cannot see how high the feeder is because only the top is visible. This is a two-dimensional (2-D) picture—a picture with length and width, but no depth.

Looking at 3-D Objects

When an object has depth as well as length and width, we say it is three-dimensional (3-D). A blown-up balloon has three dimensions. It is a 3-D object that you can hold in your hands. Let the air out of that balloon to make it flat, and you have changed a three-dimensional object into a two-dimensional shape.

Making a 3-D Model

Choose a place near your home that you know well. Look for landmarks that you think will be interesting, like a park, a church, or a pedestrian crossing. Make notes and drawings. Estimate distances by counting paces, and record the direction in which you walk. Where did you turn left or right? Which buildings are the tallest and the widest, and which shops are next to one another? Include details such as mailboxes, fences, and road signs.

Before you begin your model, find a suitable board to work on. Collect junk materials like cardboard and plastic boxes to make the buildings. Use natural materials like twigs, sticks, and stones for fences, trees, and paths. You may need to go back to check on details such as the color and shape of certain buildings.

▶ 3-D model

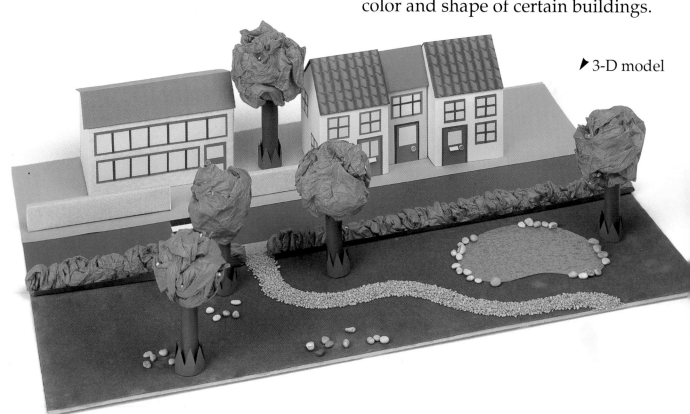

Making a Survey

Carry out a **survey** of trees or stores in your area. List the number and type of trees you see. Record the results in a picture graph, using a different symbol for each type of tree. If you carry out a store survey, draw a plan of the row of stores. Use different colors or symbols to show each kind of store. Then make a **key** for your plan.

Tree picture graph ▶

Store survey ▼

2-D plan ▶

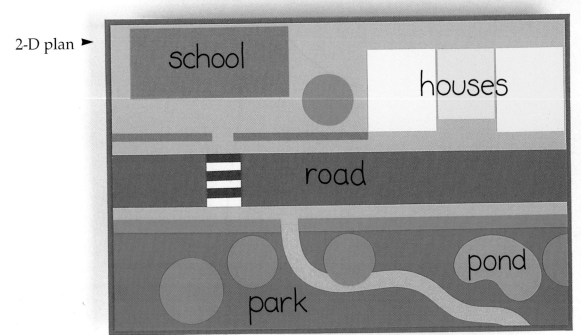

Making a 2-D Plan

When your model is finished, imagine how it would look from above—a bird's-eye view. Now draw a plan, making it as accurate as possible.

Include all the landmarks, the trees, the buildings, and the paths.
Your plan is a 2-D picture of your 3-D model.

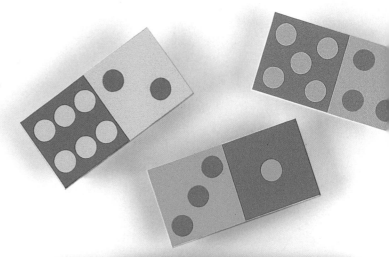

Patterns

Numbers can be shown as a pattern of dots. This is an easy way for us to recognize a number. Look at the dots on a set of dominoes—you can tell immediately what each number is. If the dots were scattered at random, it would be difficult to recognize the number. A pattern helps us to read information more easily.

Fixing Position

In a similar way, when objects are scattered at random over a surface, it is extremely difficult to describe the position of each object. If a network of squares, or **grid**, is dropped over that same collection of objects, a pattern is made. Our eyes can fix a position for each object. By numbering each row in the network and giving a letter to each column, each object can be given a letter and a number to identify its position within a particular square.

A

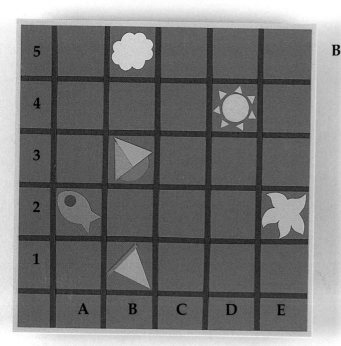

B

Look first at the collection of objects in picture *A*. Now look at picture *B*. The objects have not been moved, but you can now fix the position of each within the network of squares. Read the letter, or column, first—then the number, or row. For example, the boat is in column B, row 3, or square B3.

Where is the starfish?
Where is the flag?

The Marshall Islanders of the Pacific Ocean knew how to fix the position of their islands on a chart over 500 years ago. They studied the ocean swells and made navigation charts using sticks and shells like the one shown on the right. These charts were not taken on board their canoes, but they used the information on them to plan their journeys. Shells marked the position of each island on a network of sticks, with curves representing the pattern of the ocean swells.

Compare this map of the Canary Islands (Islas Canarias) with the shell and stick map shown below it. ▼

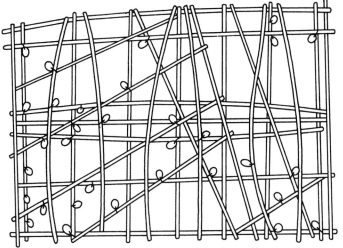

Drawing of a Marshall Island chart ▲

Make a Marshall Island Map

Look at an atlas, and choose a group of islands to chart in a way similar to that used by the Marshall Islanders. Collect straight but flexible sticks and some shells of various sizes. Criss-cross the sticks, by weaving them under and over each other, to make your network. Pick the biggest shell in your collection to represent the biggest island. Fix the position of each island by placing the shell on the appropriate part of the network.

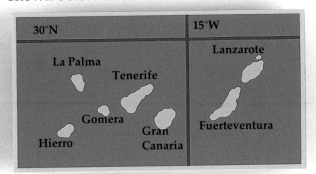

Shell and stick map of the Canary Islands

11

The Labyrinth

Labyrinths, or mazes, are made in many shapes and sizes—all have twists and turns. A maze is designed to lead people toward a particular point. Some have dead ends and are meant to confuse, like a giant puzzle. The first mazes were made out of stones or turf. The Romans made mosaic mazes.

In the Greek myth "Theseus and the Minotaur," the Minotaur—half bull, half man—lives in the center of a labyrinth. Theseus finds his way there to kill the monster. He is able to retrace his steps and escape because he has marked his route with string.

A Pebble Maze

The pebble maze below looks like the first kind of maze ever made. The original maze was a simple design of seven rings, each inside the next. You can draw a maze like this quite easily. Begin with a cross and four dots as shown below.

In the fifteenth century, people began to make garden mazes from hedges. One of the most famous, the Hampton Court Maze in London, was created at the end of the seventeenth century from yew hedges. Modern mazes have been designed in unusual shapes. There is a dragon maze and one shaped like a footprint.

➤ How to draw a pebble maze

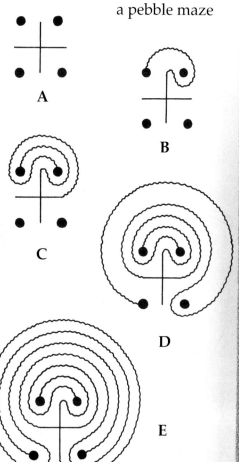

A

B

C

D

E

Pebble maze ▼

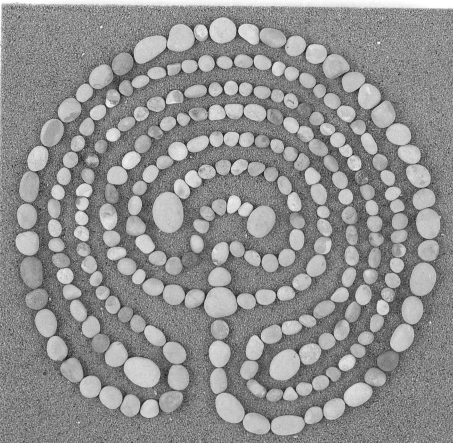

Entering a maze involves continuous movement—constantly turning left or right. It is an exciting game to play in real life, or even on paper. It is a puzzle with a solution. Because there are no landmarks, you must remember the route you have followed.

Design a Maze

You will need graph paper and a thick pen to design your maze. First, collect as many examples of maze games and pictures as you can. These will give you some good ideas. Look at the size, shape, and center point of the different mazes.

Maze design ◣

Designing a maze can be complicated. You need to plan it carefully, so make your design big. Start with any regular shape and draw thick, bold lines. Begin by drawing one pathway inside the shape. Then draw other paths leading off from the first. A detective story or a treasure hunt can be written into a maze game. Along each route you can make secret hiding places for clues that can be written in code.

Build a 3-D Maze

When your maze design is finished, drop a transparent network of squares, a grid, over it. This will enable you to enlarge your design to make a 3-D maze. You can make it as big as you like. The model shown here has been made with sticks on a sand base. What other materials would be suitable to build a maze?

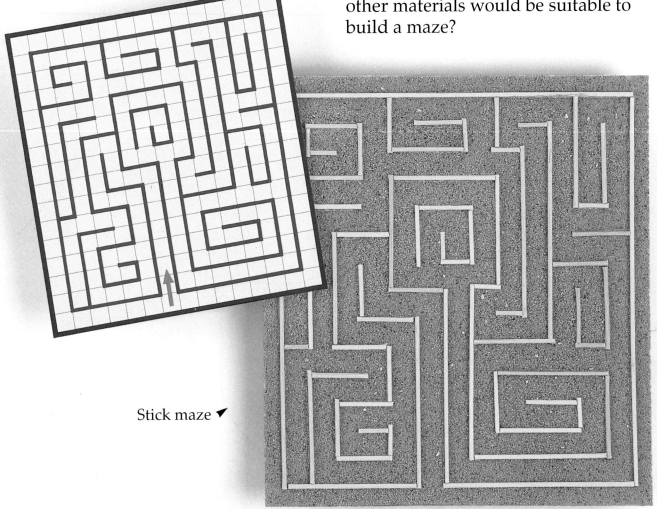

Stick maze ▼

13

When following a maze you have to turn left and right. By remembering landmarks, you can work out the way you need to travel to get from one place to another. You may need to make many changes of direction on your journey.

Nowadays, fast-moving traffic moves along a network of linked highways. Car drivers are guided by a series of road signs showing destination and direction. They have no need to look for landmarks.

Where several highways intersect, drivers must negotiate a maze of roads. One such junction has been nicknamed spaghetti junction. As in a maze, there are many possible routes. To reach a chosen destination the driver has to follow the correct road signs.

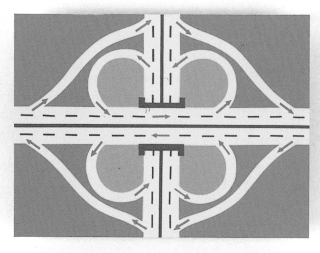

▲ A highway interchange, or spaghetti junction, can be compared to a maze.

Spaghetti Junction Maze

Create your own spaghetti junction maze game. Begin at the starting point and move around the maze, gathering points at each intersection but using each road only once. The winner is the player with the most points.

Spaghetti junction maze game ▼

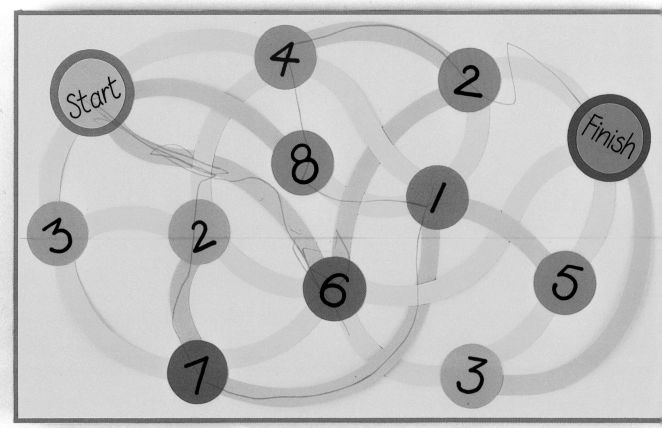

Finding Direction by Landmarks

Centuries ago, travelers used landmarks and the position of the stars to work out their direction. When the first sailors ventured out of sight of land, they had to learn to navigate without the help of landmarks. A compass became essential to establish direction.

Finding Direction by Compass

The earliest known compass was a **lodestone**—a naturally magnetic rock that when suspended always lines up north to south. Later, lodestone was used to magnetize iron needles for compasses, so that the needles would line up in the same way.

Compass rose ◣

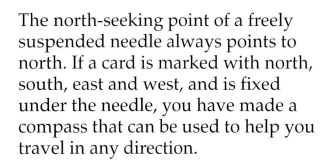

The north-seeking point of a freely suspended needle always points to north. If a card is marked with north, south, east and west, and is fixed under the needle, you have made a compass that can be used to help you travel in any direction.

▼ Fleur-de-lys template shape

Design a Compass Rose

An elaborately designed compass rose shows the positions of north, south, east, and west as on an old ship's compass. In the fifteenth century, the fleur-de-lys became the symbol for north. Look at examples of old compasses and design your own eight-point compass rose.

Design some appropriate symbols to show the four directions and think of a **mnemonic**—a rhyme or saying to remember them by.

<u>N</u>EVER, <u>E</u>VER, <u>S</u>UNNY, <u>W</u>EATHER!

S c a l e

A map is always drawn to **scale**. A picture or map drawn to scale is the same shape as the real thing, but the size is different. A plan is also called a large-scale map.

A picture of a tiny fish, drawn to scale, can be made to look larger than the real fish. A picture of a gigantic whale, drawn to scale, can be made to look smaller than the real whale. On a large-scale drawing lots of detail can be shown of something small. On a small-scale drawing less detail can be shown of something big.

Look at the pictures of a whale shown here, enlarged and reduced to scale. Choose a picture to enlarge or reduce. Decide how many squares there will be, then select the proportion to use.

Enlarging and Reducing

Using two grids you can enlarge or reduce a picture or a map. The grids, or networks, must be directly proportional in size. This means that, if you wish to make your picture twice as big, you must have the same number of squares in each. The squares on the second grid must be twice the size of the squares on the first.

1 : 2

1 : 1

2 : 1

Ratio

Scale can be shown as a ratio. A ratio of 1:2 means that the picture is half the size of the actual object. A ratio of 2:1 means that the picture is twice as big as the object. A ratio of 1:4 means that the picture is one quarter of the size of the object.

Large- and Small-Scale Maps

A large-scale map shows lots of detail, like buildings and trees. The larger the scale, the smaller the area covered by the map. A typical large-scale map is a road map.

A small-scale map shows very little detail. The smaller the scale, the larger the area covered by the map.
A map of the world is a very small-scale map.

Showing the Scale

Scale is shown on a map as a ratio or as a scale bar. A scale bar looks like this.

Scale bar ▼

On a large-scale map, 1 inch may represent 1 mile or less. On a small-scale map, 1 inch may represent 1,000 miles or more.

Rough plan showing dimensions ▼

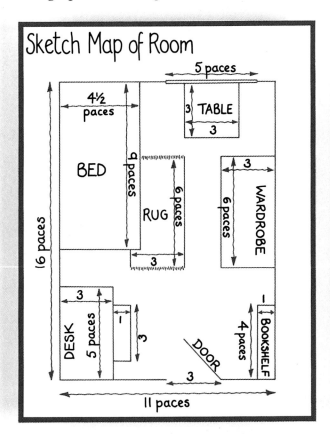

Accurate plan made to scale ▼

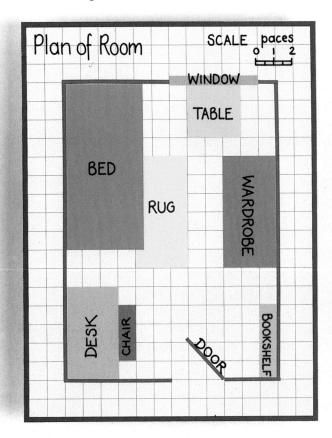

Make an Accurate Plan of a Room

Pace out the length and width of a room. Measure the dimensions of any pieces of furniture—you don't need the height because your map will be 2-D, not 3-D. Remember what you have learned about a bird's-eye view.

Is there a rug on the floor? Sketch the details roughly first, then work out an appropriate scale, for example 1 inch = 1 pace. Copy your plan onto graph paper. Remember to show the scale you have used.

Distance and direction must be accurate on any map for the map to be useful. In Britain in the sixteenth century a wooden measuring device called a "Way-Wiser" was used to measure distances. Today such distances can be measured scientifically from an airplane or satellite.

Orienteering

Following a route using a map and a compass is called **orienteering**. First you find the direction by using a compass. With your compass you can then work out the direction and **bearing** of each landmark.

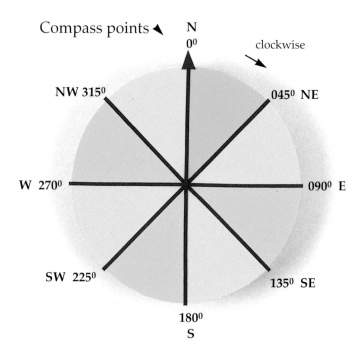

Compass points ◄

- N 0°
- clockwise
- 045° NE
- 090° E
- 135° SE
- 180° S
- SW 225°
- W 270°
- NW 315°

▲ Establishing direction on a map

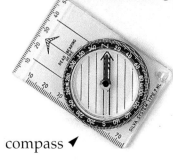

compass ◄

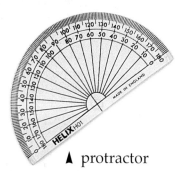

▲ protractor

Finding the Direction

Rest the compass on top of your map, making sure that the surface beneath is flat. Line up the map so that the north-seeking point of the compass is parallel with the north direction on the map. Remember that a compass needle always points to **magnetic north**. If your compass does not give bearings you must know the size of the angles between each of the compass directions. When you turn clockwise from north to face north-east you turn through an angle of 45°, or half a right angle.

Mapmaking

You can make a large-scale map of an area by looking at landmarks and calculating your distance and direction from them. Choose a familiar place, like your garden, a playground, or the local park. You will need a compass, a protractor, and some graph paper.

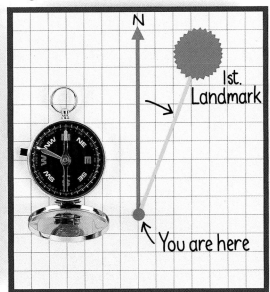

Taking a Bearing

First fix your position. Mark it clearly on the ground. This is the reference point from which all your bearings and distances are measured. Standing on that point, use the compass to find north (keep it horizontal). On the graph paper mark your position, and the direction of north. See *A*.

Face north and turn **clockwise** on the spot. Measure and record the bearings of all the interesting landmarks, using the compass. See *B*. A bearing is always measured clockwise from north and is written with 3 figures. For example, 045° means 45° east of north.

Then, from your fixed point, pace out or measure the distance to each landmark. If there is a large building take a measurement to each corner. Work out the best scale and draw the map on graph paper. Use the protractor to measure the angles accurately. Put a scale and a compass rose on your map. See *C*.

▲ Figure B   Figure C ▼

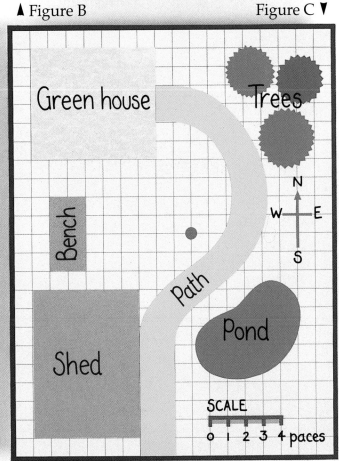

A grid over a map is a simple way of recording the position of any place or landmark. All the squares of the grid must be the same size. By printing letters or numbers in the spaces between the lines—along each axis— every square can be given a "name." This is called a **grid reference**.

National Grid

Every country has a National Grid that divides a map of the whole country into squares. Each small square covers a large area so details cannot be shown precisely.

Coordinates

On a large-scale map, like the one shown here, you can refer to the exact position of everything on the map.

To do this, the numbers must go on the lines, not the spaces between. The lines show the position east or north of a fixed point or **origin**.

Look at the church on the map below. It lies on line 7 to the east, and line 4 to the north. These numbers are the coordinates of the church.
The **easting** is written first, followed by the **northing**: (7, 4).

If a point lies between the lines, you estimate how much farther east or north the point is as a decimal. For example, the coordinates for the village pond are (5.7, 3.8).

Can you work out the coordinates for the two bridges on the map?

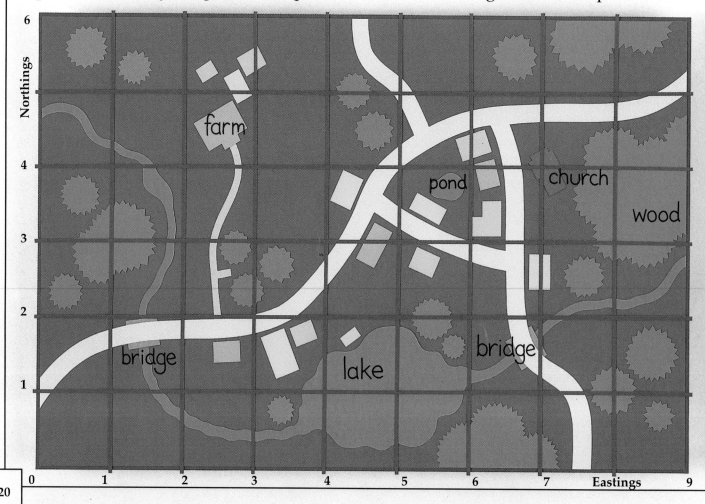

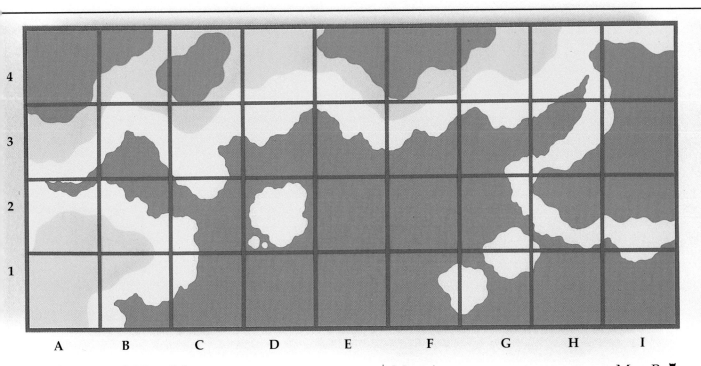

▲ Map A

Eastings and Northings

On the small-scale map, *Map A*, each square has a grid reference. Treasure Island lies in the square D2.

A large-scale map of Treasure Island, *Map B*, shows the square D2. The whole square has been divided by 10 lines running north to south and east to west to make a grid. Grid reference numbers are on the lines, not in the spaces. The grid reference for the northeast section of the lake is (D2 06 07).

On the enlarged map showing part of the island, *Map C,* you can be even more exact. Imagine another grid has been drawn inside the square in which the section of the lake lies. You can now pinpoint the buried treasure by giving its position east of the easting and north of the northing. The 6 figure grid reference is (062 078).

Treasure Hunt

Draw a Treasure Island map and make up a treasure hunt for your friends, giving only coordinates as the clues.

Map B ▼

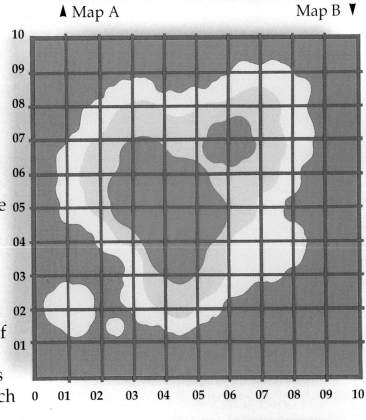

Map C ►

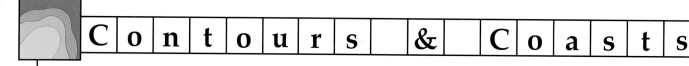

All maps show position and direction. A map that also shows the shape or **relief** of the land is called a **topographical** map.

Contours

Because a map is 2-dimensional, height and depth are shown by shading, layer-coloring, or numbered lines called **contours**. Layer-coloring is usually used to show **altitude** on a small-scale map. A key explains the height or depth represented by each color.

Contours are lines joining places of the same height. They are used on large-scale maps. All measurements are given as height above sea level.

Where contour lines are close together, there is a steep slope. If they are farther apart the slope is more gradual. When contours stop suddenly at the coast, a steep cliff is indicated.

Shading is sometimes used to show height. The effect is 3-dimensional but does not show exact heights. **Spot heights** give the exact height at a precise point.

Find a large-scale map that has contours marked on it. Find a river valley, and follow the route of the river downhill, looking at the contour lines. Where do you think the river flows fastest? What tells you that the river flows quickly there?

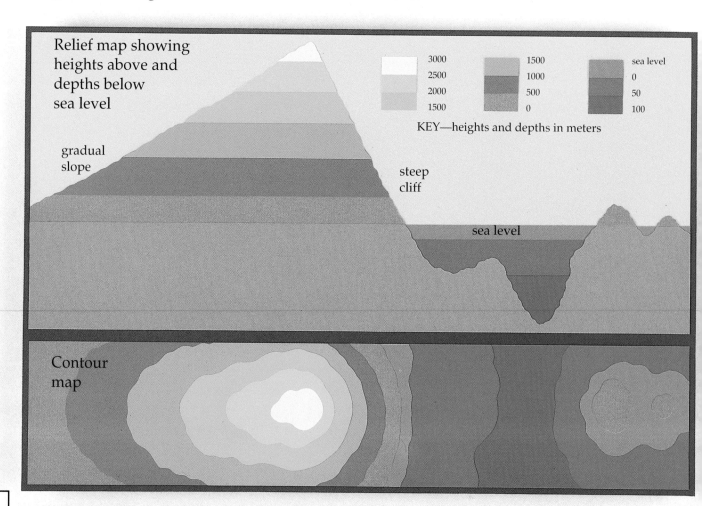

Relief map showing heights above and depths below sea level

gradual slope

steep cliff

sea level

3000	1500	sea level
2500	1000	0
2000	500	50
1500	0	100

KEY—heights and depths in meters

Contour map

Sea level

The ocean bed has mountains, valleys, and volcanoes just like the land.
To measure depth below sea level, we use an echo sounder. It gives a picture of the shape of the sea bed. The echo sounder sends pulses of sound through the water. The pulses strike the sea bed and bounce back as echoes. Sound travels through water at about 5,000 feet per second. So, by measuring the time it takes the echoes to return, we can learn how deep the water is.

Scientists have been able to map much of the ocean floor. But they are still learning more about it.

Coasts

A landlocked country has no coastline. Those countries that have a coastline need to map its shape precisely—it is part of the relief of that country.
A sailors' map showing coastlines and water depths is called a chart.
A long time ago the Inuit in Greenland devised a way of recording the shape of their coastline by carving relief maps from wood.

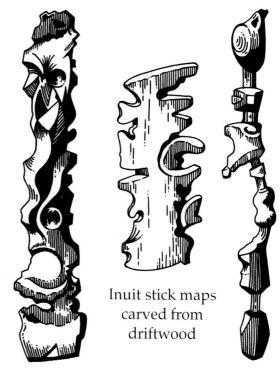

Inuit stick maps
carved from
driftwood

Make a String Map

Choose a country. Shape its outline from memory using a length of string. Check with an atlas to see how accurate your string map is and correct the shape if necessary.

Shape a Coastline

Look in an atlas and choose a stretch of coastline or an island. Make a stick map using modeling clay. Can your friends recognize the shape?

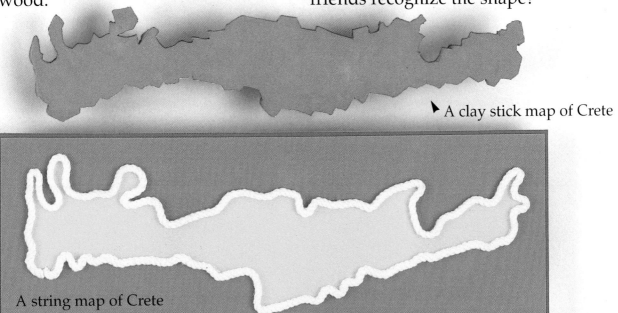

▶ A clay stick map of Crete

A string map of Crete

On maps and globes, the Earth is divided by a grid of lines running east to west and north to south. Those running east to west are lines of **latitude**. Those running north to south are lines of **longitude**.

The **equator** is the line of zero latitude, and the **Greenwich**, or prime, **meridian** is the line of zero longitude.

Lines of latitude and longitude allow us to fix coordinates for the position of any landmark on the surface of the Earth. Where the equator and the prime meridian cross, just off the coast of central Africa, is the fixed point from which navigation all over the world is calculated.

Latitude

Lines of latitude tell us how far north or south of the equator we are. They are parallel to the equator and are named by the imaginary angle they make at the center of the Earth. You can see in the diagram how this is calculated.

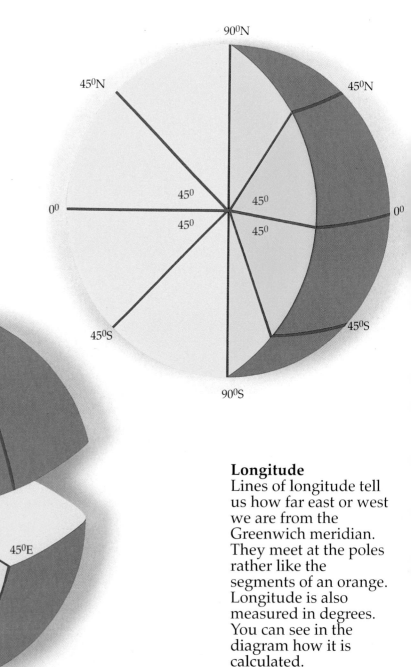

Longitude

Lines of longitude tell us how far east or west we are from the Greenwich meridian. They meet at the poles rather like the segments of an orange. Longitude is also measured in degrees. You can see in the diagram how it is calculated.

Longitude and Time

The Earth spins on an axis that runs through the north and south poles. We base our idea of time on the position of the sun. If it is midday where we are standing, then to the west of us it is still morning, and to the east it is already afternoon.

The Earth takes 24 hours to spin around once. That is to spin through 360°. In one hour it spins through 15°. When traveling west, for every 15° you must turn back your watch one hour.

To make life simpler, we have divided the Earth into time zones. The time at the prime meridian is called **Greenwich Mean Time**. There are 12 time zones going westward and 12 time zones going eastward. They meet at the international date line.

Telling the Time

Look at a map of the world. Find the prime meridian. What is the time around the world if it is 12 noon at Greenwich? What happens to the date when you cross the international date line?

Map showing time around the world ▼

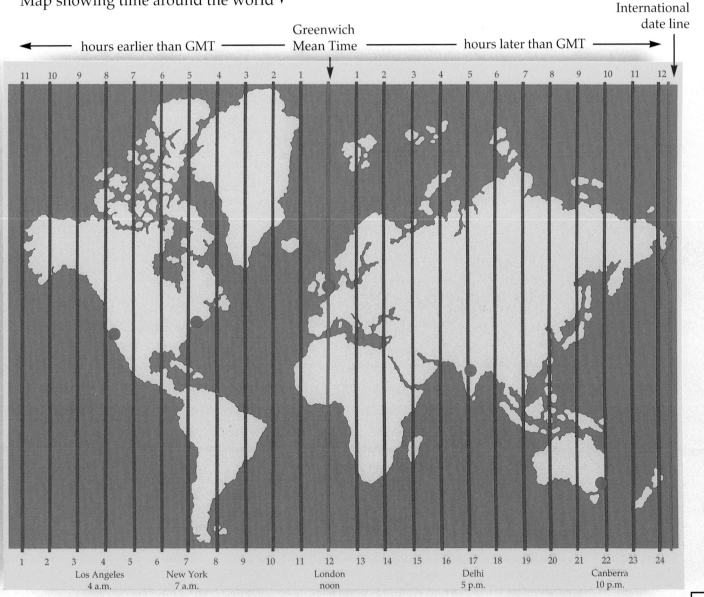

Marks With a Meaning

To convey information without words we use signs. A sign is a mark that has a particular meaning that we all understand. Signs may represent values, words, phrases, or ideas.

Pictograms and Ideograms

A sign may be a simplified picture, or pictogram. On a large-scale map or plan of a park, you could show the position of trees by drawing tree pictograms. A sign may be an idea picture, or ideogram. An object is drawn that represents something abstract—an idea that cannot be touched. The dove is recognized all over the world as a sign of peace.

Using a Key

Using signs helps to simplify the information on a map, making it clear and easy to understand. Every map should have a key, or legend, explaining the meaning of the signs used. The key shown opposite explains the signs used on a weather map. Without the key the map would be meaningless.

Mapping the Weather

Observe the weather over a period of time. Record the hours of sunshine, the strength of the wind, and the types of clouds. Design some weather symbols of your own and record your results on a chart.

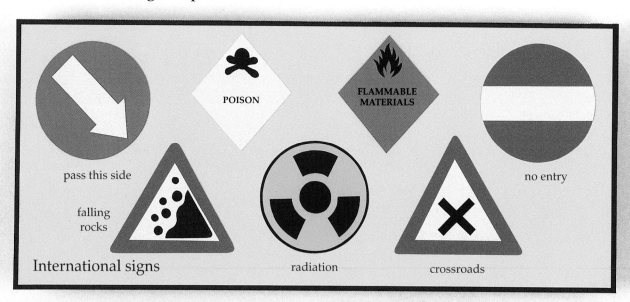

pass this side

falling rocks

International signs

POISON

FLAMMABLE MATERIALS

radiation

no entry

crossroads

Symbols

A symbol may bear little resemblance to what it symbolizes. Many large organizations and companies have their own symbol, called a logo. Logos are usually very simple, but are important as identification marks. The Olympic Games logo is recognized all over the world.

International Signs

Certain signs, such as road signs, are international. Road signs must be easily understood because they give instructions and warnings to drivers. A road may be used by people of many nationalities. The signs used must be standardized as far as possible.

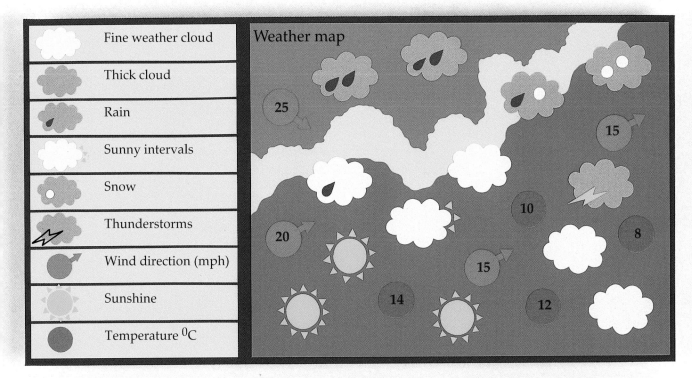

Fine weather cloud	
Thick cloud	
Rain	
Sunny intervals	
Snow	
Thunderstorms	
Wind direction (mph)	
Sunshine	
Temperature ^{0}C	

Weather map

Using Signs

Design a key of original symbols to show details of pollution on a map of the world. Think of appropriate signs to show the problems of acid rain, poor air quality, and oil spillage.

Make an "environmentally friendly" map of your locality. Use signs to represent recycling collection points. Include trash cans and mark litter as "black spots."

Tracking Signs

Before all the land had been explored and mapped, people on the move sent scouts to explore the land ahead. The scouts laid trails, making signs using the natural materials around, so that others could follow.

Think up a series of tracking signs with your friends. Then lay a trail through woodland or a park. See if your friends can find you.

▼ Tracking signs

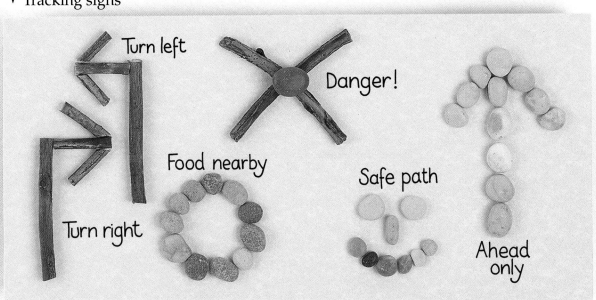

S h a p e & S i z e

Countries

A country is a territory with a national boundary. To travel from one country to another usually requires a special document such as a passport. From an atlas we can learn the shape and size of every country in the world.

Continents

A continent is a large land mass, usually containing a number of countries. The world's seven continents are Africa, North America, South America, Antarctica, Asia, Europe, and Australasia. Asia is the largest continent and covers almost one third of the Earth.

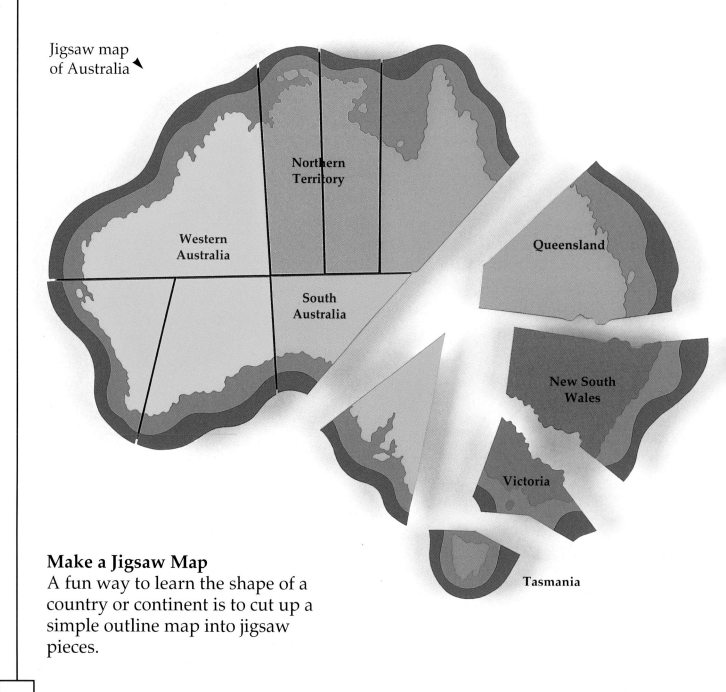

Jigsaw map of Australia

Northern Territory

Western Australia

South Australia

Queensland

New South Wales

Victoria

Tasmania

Make a Jigsaw Map

A fun way to learn the shape of a country or continent is to cut up a simple outline map into jigsaw pieces.

Shapes and Sizes

Some countries have a distinctive shape. The shape of France looks like a hexagon, and Italy resembles a heeled boot. Years ago lighthearted caricature maps of various countries were popular as a source of amusement.

Shape a Country

Choose any country that has a distinctive shape, and design a picture to fit inside its outline. Does its shape suggest anything to you—a picture of a face or an animal?

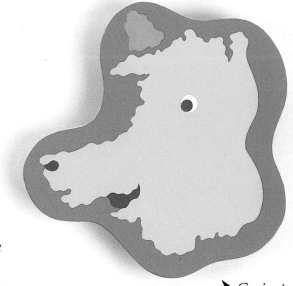

▸ Caricature map of Wales, in Great Britain

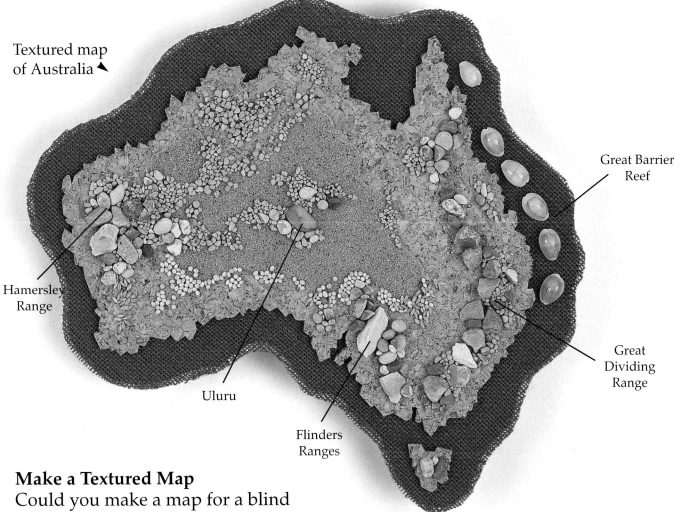

Textured map of Australia ◂

Great Barrier Reef

Great Dividing Range

Hamersley Range

Uluru

Flinders Ranges

Make a Textured Map

Could you make a map for a blind person to use? Think about using different textures to convey important details and information.

A map tells us a great deal about a country, or area, without using words. An information map has immediate impact, unlike pages of text. Maps have been used throughout the centuries to guide and inform.

Thematic Maps

Thematic maps give very specific information that can be seen at a glance. A population map shows immediately which country has the most people per square mile.

Make a Food Map

You can make a thematic map of where the food in your local supermarket comes from. Pick one continent—for example, Europe. Collect as many food labels as possible from packages and cans—be sure they are of European origin. Trace or enlarge an outline map of Europe and invent a way of showing which countries the foods come from. You could also add capital cities and national flags, and show which countries are members of the European Community (EC).

▲ Thematic map showing foods from Europe

Make a Flag Map

Each country has a national flag that is recognized the world over. At the opening ceremony of the Olympic Games, the flags of all the nations taking part are carried in procession.

The United States flag is the Stars and Stripes. Its thirteen red and white stripes represent the original thirteen states, and its fifty stars represent the states today.

Find out about other national and international flags, and use your information to make a flag map for a single continent or the whole world.

Linear Maps

Linear maps like the ones shown on this page were once used to show postal routes in Great Britain. These maps were narrow strips that showed in great detail the countryside around one main road. They could be rolled up and carried in a pocket. The postal maps were unrolled and read from the bottom up to the top. The direction of each strip was shown by a compass rose.

Make a Linear Map

Choose a road or river route and draw it as a linear map. Or make a linear map of a route you travel often—from your home to school or to a friend's home, for example. Show important landmarks along the way, and include a compass rose with north shown correctly.

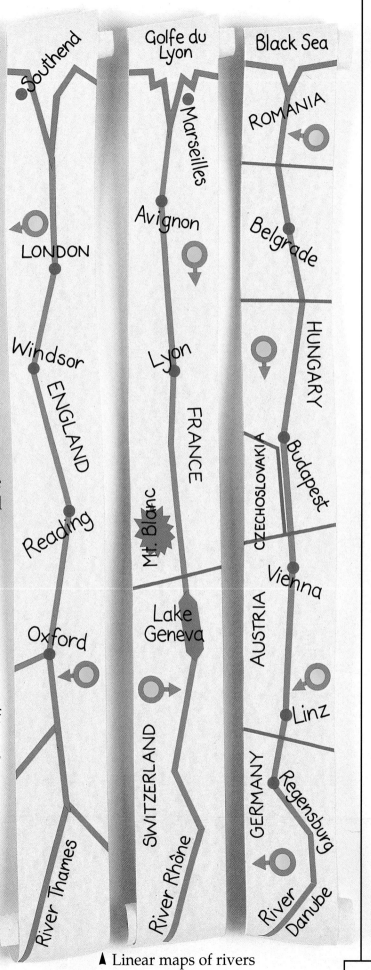

▲ Linear maps of rivers

Altitude Height above sea level.

Atlas A book of charts or maps.

Axis An imaginary line around which the Earth rotates. Also a line of reference on a grid. Plural: axes.

Bearing The compass direction of a point, shown in degrees from north.

Chart A map used to navigate by sea or air.

Clockwise Moving in the same direction as the hands of a clock.

Contour A line on a map joining places of the same height or depth.

Coordinates A set of numbers describing the position of a point with reference to a system of axes.

Easting A map coordinate giving position east of the point of origin.

Elliptical orbit The shape, like a flattened circle, of the path the Earth takes as it travels around the Sun.

Equator An imaginary line around the Earth, midway between the poles—the line of $0°$ latitude.

Fleur-de-lys A heraldic symbol—a lily with three petals.

Geographic north and south poles The two points on the Earth's surface where lines of longitude cross.

Greenwich Mean Time (GMT) The time at the prime meridian. Time zones east of Greenwich are ahead of GMT; those to the west are behind.

Greenwich meridian The line of $0°$ longitude—also known as the prime meridian.

Grid A network of horizontal and vertical lines, placed on a map for locating points.

Grid reference The name given to each square in a grid.

International date line An imaginary line approximately $180°$ W. When crossing from west to east, you go back by 24 hours.

Key A list of explanations of symbols and code—also known as a legend.

Landmark A prominent feature.

Latitude Imaginary lines parallel to the equator by which you can fix your position north or south.

Lodestone A naturally magnetic rock.

Longitude Imaginary lines at right angles to the equator by which you can fix your position east or west of the prime meridian.

Magnetic north The place on the Earth's surface toward which a magnetic needle points.

Mnemonic A saying or other device to improve memory.

Northing A map coordinate giving position north of the origin.

Orienteering Using a map and compass to follow a route.

Origin A fixed point from which map coordinates are numbered.

Plan A drawing or diagram showing a top or horizontal view.

Relief The shape of the land.

Scale The relationship between actual distance and distance on a map.

Sphere A round object, like a ball.

Spot height A point of known height marked on a map.

Survey A collection of information about some aspect of an area.

Topographical Showing land features.